Hop in the Van, Quin!

By Carmel Reilly

Quin sat on his bed.

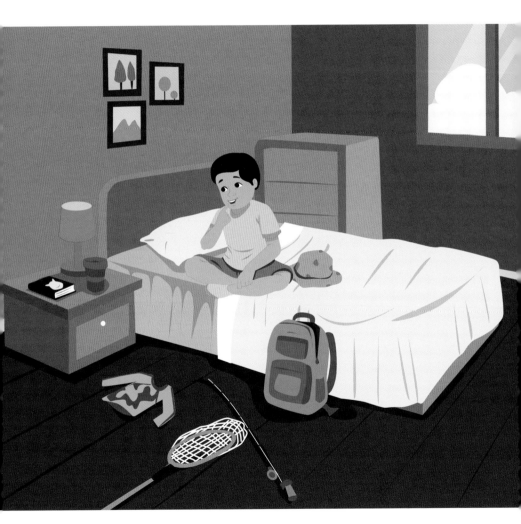

Hop in the van, kids!

Let me get my rod and net kit, too.

Quin pops on his sun top
and sun hat.

Mum, it is **not** a lot!

CHECKING FOR MEANING

1. What does Quin try to pack in his bag? *(Literal)*

2. What did Viv carry for Quin? *(Literal)*

3. What time of year do you think the story is set in? Why? *(Inferential)*

EXTENDING VOCABULARY

lid	Look at the word *lid*. What words can you think of that rhyme with this word?
too	The word *too* means *also* or *as well*. *To* and *two* sound the same as *too*. What do each of these words mean?
hop	What does the word *hop* mean in the story? What other words could be used instead of *hop* in the sentence *Hop in the van*?

MOVING BEYOND THE TEXT

1. Where do you think Quin and Viv might have been going for a dip?

2. What do you like to do when it is hot?

3. What are some ways you should protect yourself when you go out in the sun?

4. What would you take with you if you were going to the beach?

SPEED SOUNDS

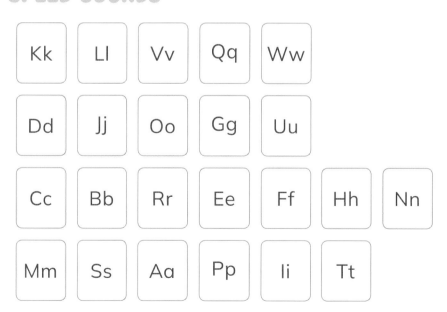

Kk	Ll	Vv	Qq	Ww		
Dd	Jj	Oo	Gg	Uu		
Cc	Bb	Rr	Ee	Ff	Hh	Nn
Mm	Ss	Aa	Pp	Ii	Tt	

PRACTICE WORDS

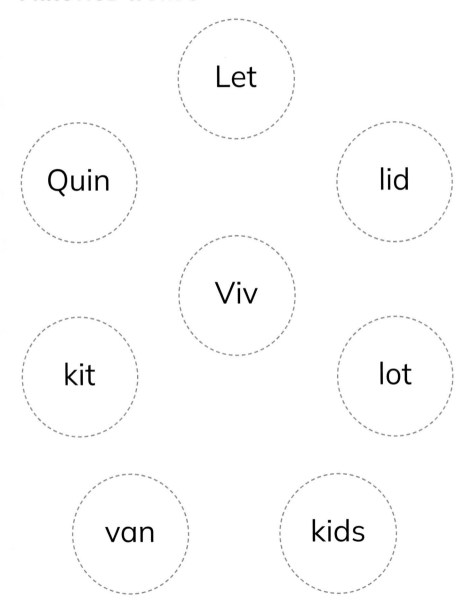

Let

Quin

lid

Viv

kit

lot

van

kids